Contents

Fairy notepaper

Print your own special writing paper and notepaper. Decorate it with pretty coloured fairies and a sprinkling of fairy dust.

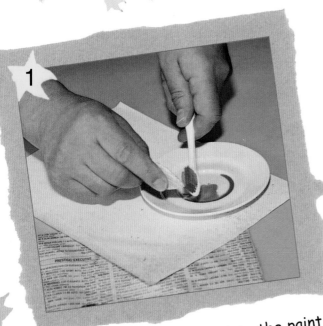

1. Dip an old toothbrush into the paint. Carefully drag a piece of stiff card across the bristles to splatter paint over one bottom corner of a sheet of paper.

2. Using template A on page 28, trace the fairy onto the corrugated cardboard. Now cut the fairy shape into nine separate shapes i.e. arms, wings, legs, etc.

3. Paint the fairy's body and place it paint side down on your paper as shown. Press down firmly before carefully lifting it off.

You will need:

Corrugated cardboard
Scissors
Poster paint
Paintbrush
Old toothbrush
A4 size sheets of white or pale coloured paper
Felt-tip pens
Gold paint

4

4. Use a different colour to paint and print her face, arms and legs. Choose another colour for her wings.

5. Draw her face on with felt-tip pens and paint her hair. Decorate her dress too. When everything is dry your notepaper is ready to use.

Magic fairy writing

You will need:

Lemon juice
Saucer
Thin paintbrush
White paper
Warm radiator

1

1. Squeeze some lemon juice into a saucer. Dip your paintbrush in it and write out your message.

2. When your message is dry, hold it near a radiator. As it warms up, your writing will appear as if by magic!

5

Fairy beads

These paper beads are easy to make and look stunning. Create your own fabulous fairy necklace and bangle.

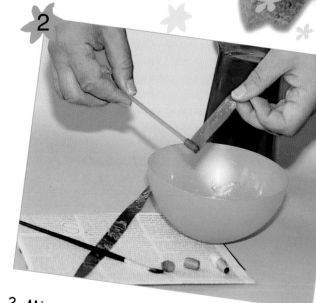

1. To make the beads, cut magazine pages and coloured paper into thin strips (1.5 cm x 40 cm). Then cut each strip so that one end narrows to a point.

2. Mix some glue and water in a bowl and use to cover a paper strip. Smear a straw with washing-up liquid. Roll the paper strip tightly around the straw, starting at the widest end.

3. Gently slip the bead off the straw and leave to dry. Make more beads in the same way using magazine and white paper strips.

You will need:

White glue
An old bowl
A plastic straw
Washing-up liquid
Old paintbrush (to apply glue)
Old magazines
Purple and white coloured paper
Scissors
Pink or purple netting
Ribbon or string

Make different size beads by using wider or longer strips of paper. Make an extra large bead and paint tiny flowers on it.

4

4. Decide which bead you want in the centre of your necklace and arrange the others on either side of it. Thread them onto ribbon. Strips of coloured netting can also be threaded between the beads. Make extra beads for a matching necklace and bangle set.

Fairy picture album

Treasure your favourite pictures in this
fabulous fairy album. Decorate it with
delicate pressed flowers, gilded leaves
and ribbons.

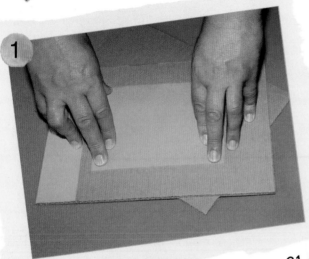

1. Cut a strip of pink card (5 cm x 21 cm)
and glue it onto the left side of one piece
of corrugated cardboard. Cut another
piece of pink card (13 cm x 17 cm) and
glue it to the centre.

2. Cut a square of fabric fur (7cm x
7cm). Now cut it in half diagonally to
make two triangles. Glue fur
triangles onto the other corners.

To press a flower: lay it
carefully between two sheets
of kitchen roll or blotting paper.
Put a pile of books on top for a week
or two so the flower is flattened
and dried out.

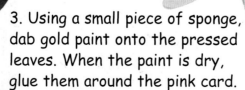

3. Using a small piece of sponge,
dab gold paint onto the pressed
leaves. When the paint is dry,
glue them around the pink card.

You will need

Two A4 pieces of corrugated
  cardboard
One A4 sheet of pink card or paper
Flowers and leaves to press
Pink fabric fur
Pink ribbon (approx. 40 cm)
Hole punch
Glue
Scissors
Gold paint
Small piece of sponge
A4 sheets of pale pink, blue
  and purple paper

8

4. Glue dried flowers among the leaves. Decorate the centre of your album cover with more flowers or paper shapes to create a flower fairy picture.

5. Using a hole punch make two holes in the left side of both pieces of corrugated cardboard. Make holes in several sheets of coloured paper in exactly the same place.

6. Sandwich the paper between the cardboard. Now thread ribbon through the holes and tie a bow. Glue circles of fur to the ribbon ends.

Fairy wand

Weave magical spells with this funky fairy wand. Wave your wand to make a trail of glittering, star-sprinkled fairy dust.

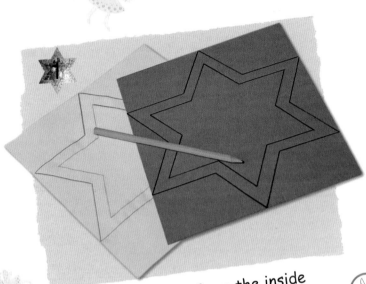

1. Use template Q from the inside front cover. Draw a large star with a smaller star inside onto corrugated card. Cut around the large star. Don't throw the leftover card away!

2. Cut gold and silver paper into small triangles, squares and rectangles. Leaving tiny gaps between each piece, glue silver paper onto the small star and gold around the edge.

You will need:

Corrugated cardboard (20 cm x 23.5 cm)
  plus cardboard scraps
Gold paper
Silver paper or aluminium foil
Scissors
Ruler
Felt-tip pen or pencil
Sticky tape
Glue
Pink ribbon (the type used for gift wrapping)
Thin garden cane (approx. 36 cm)

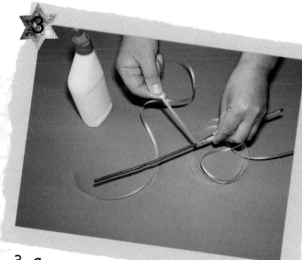

3. Cover the cane with glue and wind pink ribbon around it. When dry, attach the cane to the back of the star with sticky tape.

Wave your wand three times to make a wish or four times to cast a spell!

4. Glue gold and silver paper onto the leftover card. Use template R from the inside cover to draw six stars on the card. Cut out and glue them onto two lengths of ribbon.

5. Stick the ribbons onto the back of your wand with tape.

11

Fairy frame

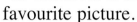

Create a wonderful woodland fairy frame. It is the perfect place for your favourite picture.

1. Draw a rectangle (15 cm x 10 cm) in the middle of the sheet of cardboard. Place the strips of cardboard around it and glue them in place.

2. Now paint the strips of cardboard gold.

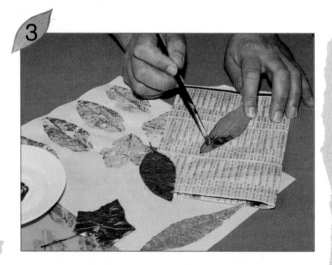

3. Paint a leaf gold. Place it paint side down on coloured paper and press down firmly. Peel the leaf off. Use different shaped leaves to make more prints.

You will need:

One sheet corrugated cardboard (24 cm x 28 cm)
Four strips corrugated cardboard
   (two 1.5 cm x 15 cm and two 1.5 cm x 10 cm)
Ruler
Felt-tip pen or pencil
Glue
Pale blue and purple paper
Leaves
Four skeleton leaves (from a craft shop, optional)
Gold paint
Thin card (15 cm x 15 cm, to paint gold)
Paintbrush
Scissors

4. When dry, cut out the leaf prints and glue them to your frame.

5. Glue four skeleton leaves or gold-painted leaves onto gold card and cut them out. Now glue one to each corner of your frame.

You could also add some gold stars or shiny fabric cut into leaf shapes. When everything is dry, display a picture in the frame.

13

Fairy wings

Silver wings will complete any fairy outfit. When you put them on remember to move gracefully like a fairy and to walk on tiptoe.

1. Place a dinner plate on the cardboard (as shown) and draw around it. Now draw a simple wing shape to fill the remaining space. Cut out this wing and use it as a template for the other piece of card. Cut out the second wing.

2. Spread glue over the front of one wing and place it glue side down onto the dull side of the foil. When dry, cut off the extra foil. Repeat with the other wing.

3. Use templates C, D and E on page 28 to draw heart, flower and star shapes onto some thin card. Tear magazine pictures into small pieces. Glue these to your shapes and cut them out.

You will need:

Two large sheets corrugated cardboard
 (38 cm x 26 cm)
Dinner plate
Felt-tip pen or pencil
One square piece corrugated cardboard
 (12 cm x 12 cm)
Hole punch
Scissors
Aluminium foil
Old magazines
Thin card
Glue
Two pieces of ribbon (each 160 cm long)

14

5. Using a hole punch, make two holes on each side of the cardboard square. Thread a ribbon through each pair of holes.

4. Glue the heart, flower and star shapes onto both wings.

7. Tie the ribbons round your waist and under your arms. Now flutter your fairy wings and fly!

6. Lay the wings face down and side by side. Glue the square of card over the centre join (as shown), the ribbons on top.

15

Fairy mobile

Beautiful butterflies decorate this wonderful fairy mobile. Hang it by a window to see it shine and flutter in the breeze.

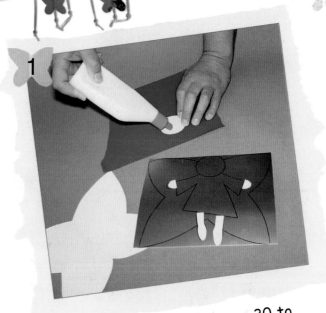

1. Use template F on page 30 to draw a fairy onto gold card. Trace the fairy's face, hands and legs onto white card. Cut them out and glue them on.

2. Paint the arms, legs and face. Fold each piece of wool in half and glue them to her head. Carefully tear coloured paper to create the dress.

3. Glue pretty scraps of fabric onto her dress. Cut pink and purple card into heart shapes to glue onto her wings. Cut out your fairy.

You will need:

A piece of gold card (22 cm x 18 cm)

Thin card: white, pink and purple

Coloured paper

Felt-tip pen or a pencil

Eight pieces of yellow wool (approx. 20 cm)

Seven pieces of ribbon (approx. 40 cm)

Glue and sticky tape

Scissors

Hole punch

Scraps of fabric

Poster paint

Paintbrush

4. Using a hole punch make one hole in the top and three holes along the bottom of each wing.

5. Use template G on page 29 to trace butterfly shapes onto thin, coloured card. Cut out and glue them onto the strands of ribbon.

6. Thread a ribbon through each hole at the base of the wings and tape it at the back. Add a loop of ribbon at the top in the same way.

Fairy pop-up card

Amaze your friends and family when you
give them this lovely pop-up fairy card.

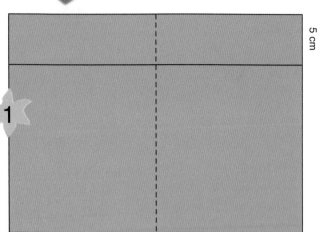

1

5 cm

1. Fold the card in half as shown. Draw
a line across it, 5 cm below the top edge.

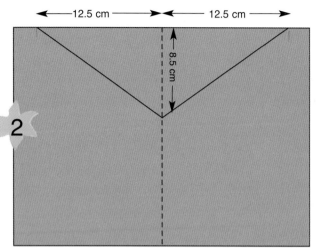

←— 12.5 cm —→←— 12.5 cm —→

8.5 cm

2

2. Turn the card over. Measure 12.5 cm
each side from the centre fold.
Measure 8.5 cm down the centre fold
and draw lines to join up these points.

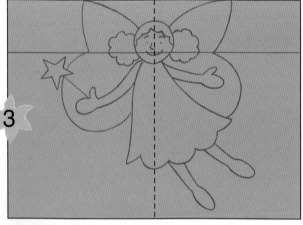

3

3. Turn the card over. Use template H
on page 30. The tracing guideline should
sit on the centre fold with the wings
touching the top edge. Trace the fairy.

4

4. Cut away the top section
of the card, above the line.
Take care cutting around the
fairy's head and wings.

You will need:

Pink card (A4)
Ruler
Felt-tip pens
Pencil

Paintbrush
Poster paints
Gold paint
Scissors

18

5. Fold the card, gently pushing the fairy's head and wings into the fold as it closes. Crease the line folds well.

6. Paint your fairy using poster paints. Use gold paint for her wings and wand. Paint her face, or draw it with felt-tip pens.

Paint flowers on the fairy dress and around the card. Or you could use a stencil (see step 7).

7. Use templates I, J and K on page 30 to draw three stencils on thin card. Once you have cut the shapes out place them on the fairy card and dab paint over them.

19

Fairy tiara

Become a beautiful fairy wearing this stunning tiara.

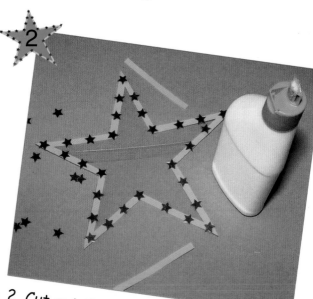

1. Use template L on page 31 to draw a star shape on white paper. Cut it out and tape it to the plastic. Now cut away the plastic around the star template.

2. Cut out thin strips of blue paper (6 mm x 8 cm). Glue these around the edges of the plastic star and stick silver stars to them.

3. Place the cardboard strip around your head. Ask an adult to tape the strip so that it fits. Cut off the extra card.

You will need:

Stiff clear plastic (18 cm x 18 cm)
Thin cardboard (2.5 cm x 46 cm)
White paper
Blue or turquoise paper
Sticky tape
Glue
Sticky silver stars
Scraps of fabric
Blue netting (15 cm x 50 cm)

20

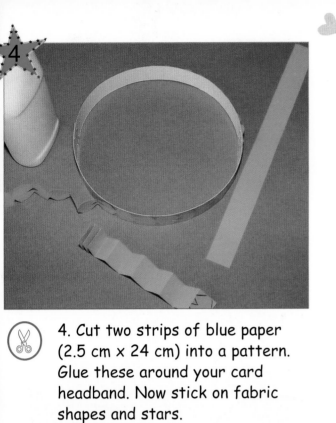

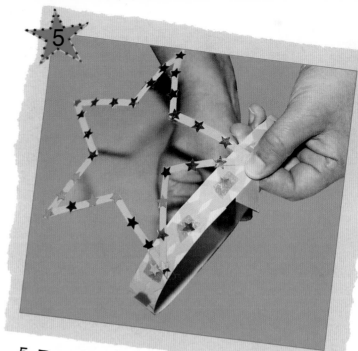

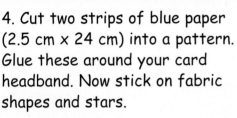 4. Cut two strips of blue paper (2.5 cm x 24 cm) into a pattern. Glue these around your card headband. Now stick on fabric shapes and stars.

5. Tape the star onto the front of the band. Gather up the netting and glue it to the band, behind the star.

6. Finish your tiara with a paper or fabric heart shape (template M on page 31) glued in the centre of the star.

Fairy decoration

This fantastic fairy looks wonderful wherever she stands! She could even decorate the top of a Christmas tree.

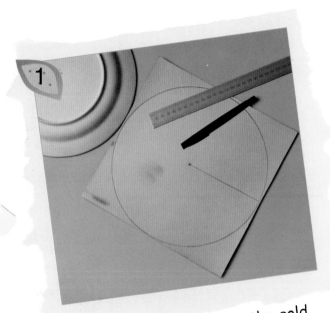

1. Place a dinner plate on the gold card and draw round it. Cut the circle out. Draw a straight line from the centre of the circle to the edge, then cut along it.

2. Overlap the straight edges of your card to make a cone. Hold it in place with sticky tape.

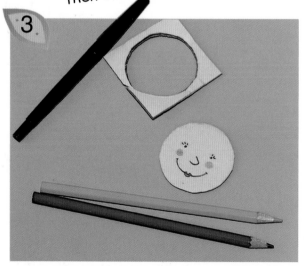

3. Place an egg cup on thick card, draw around it and cut out the circle. Paint the fairy's face then draw on her eyes, nose and mouth.

You will need:

Thin gold card (40 cm x 30 cm)
Thick card (5 cm x 5 cm)
Purple paper
Yellow paper strips (20 cm x .5 mm)
Two round paper doilies
Ruler
Felt-tip pen
Poster paints or crayons
Scissors
Sticky tape
Glue
Gold stars
Egg cup
Dinner plate

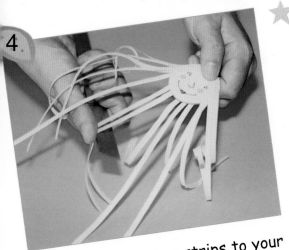

4

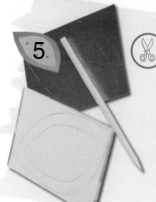

5

5. Using template N on page 31 trace a wing onto gold card. Flip the template over before tracing the second wing. Cut out both wings and decorate them with coloured paper and stars.

4. Glue yellow paper strips to your fairy's head. Give her curly hair by dragging the edge of a ruler along each strip of paper.

6

8. Cut the lace edging from the paper doylies. Glue it to the base of the cone and decorate the fairy with purple paper stars. Make her wand from a thin strip of card and a gold star (template O on page 31).

6. Glue your fairy's head near the top of the cone. Then tape both wings onto the back.

7

7. Cut two triangles of gold card (5 cm x 9 cm x 9 cm) for arms. Cut two small semicircles of card for hands and glue them to the bottom of the triangles. Glue the arms in place. Cut out a crown from the gold card and glue it onto her head.

Fairy cakes

Bake these scrumptious cakes. Make pretty pink icing and decorate the cakes with hundreds and thousands. Now invite your friends to tea!

1. Ask an adult to turn on the oven at 180°C, (Gas Mark 4). Mix the butter and sugar together in a large bowl until it is creamy. Add the egg and beat well.

2. Carefully fold in the flour. Place 12 paper cases in a bun tray. Spoon equal amounts of cake mixture into each one.

3. Ask an adult to put your cakes in the middle of the oven for 12-15 minutes, or until golden brown and well risen. Take them out and leave to cool.

You will need:

Two mixing bowls
Bun tray or baking sheet
Wooden spoon

To make 12 fairy cakes:
75 g butter
75 g caster sugar
One egg
75 g self-raising flour
12 paper cases

For the icing:
50 g butter or margarine
Icing sugar
2-3 drops of pink food colouring
Hundreds and thousands

24

Icing!

4. Put the butter into a small bowl and stir in the icing sugar. Add the pink food colouring and mix well.

5. Ask an adult to help you cut the rounded tops off some of your cakes. Cut each one in half to create 'wings'.

6. Drop a spoonful of icing into each hollow and pop the fairy wings on top.

7. Spread pink icing over the uncut cakes and sprinkle with hundreds and thousands, like fairy dust.

Fairy puppet

This fairy finger puppet moves her head and waves her magic wand. She has long hair and a gorgeous golden dress. Make puppets with all your friends and put on a fairy play.

1. Fold the white paper in half and use to trace template S. Cut it out and tape the template to the gold card to draw around the shape.

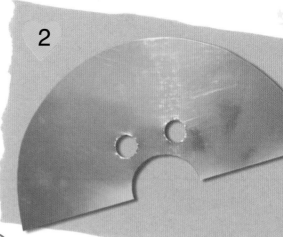

2. Cut around the outside of the shape. Use an old ball-point pen to make a small hole in the centre of each of the two circles. This will make it easier to cut out the circles.

3. Overlap the straight edges of the gold card to make a cone shape with a hole in the centre. Then use tape to hold it together.

You will need:

Gold card (30 cm x 15 cm)
Thin white paper (30 cm x 15 cm)
Coloured card: pink, purple or blue
Felt-tip pen or pencil
Poster paint
Scissors
Yellow wool
Scraps of netting and fabric
Glue
Sticky tape
Gold and silver stars
Cotton bud
Old ball-point pen
Mug or cup

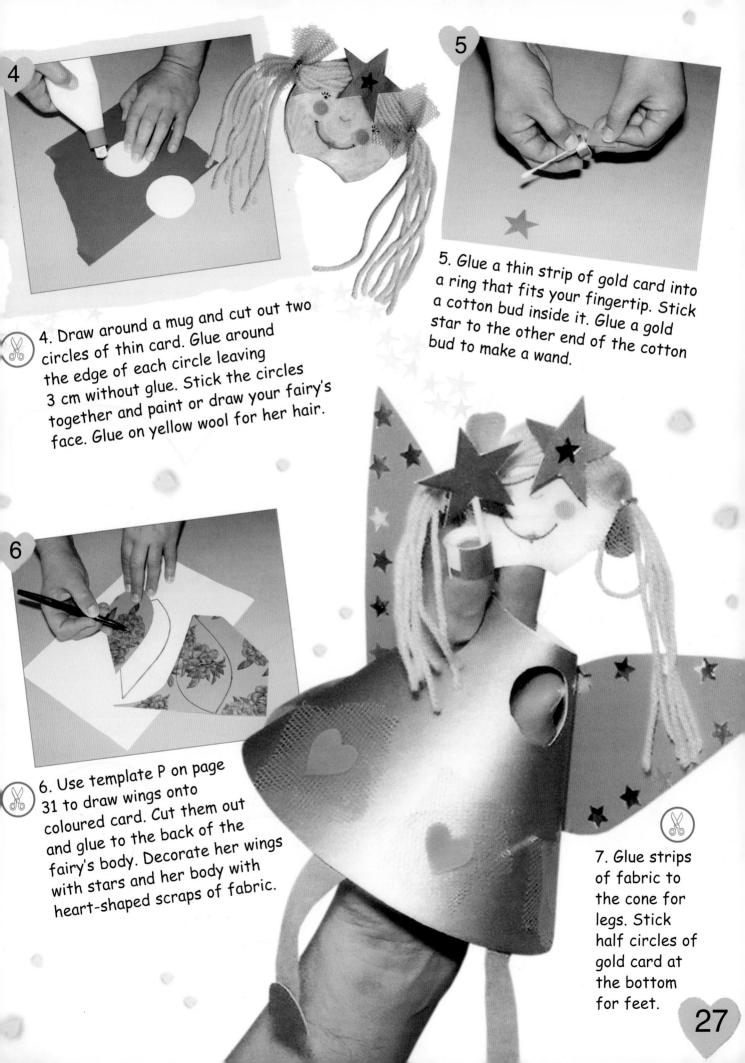

4. Draw around a mug and cut out two circles of thin card. Glue around the edge of each circle leaving 3 cm without glue. Stick the circles together and paint or draw your fairy's face. Glue on yellow wool for her hair.

5. Glue a thin strip of gold card into a ring that fits your fingertip. Stick a cotton bud inside it. Glue a gold star to the other end of the cotton bud to make a wand.

6. Use template P on page 31 to draw wings onto coloured card. Cut them out and glue to the back of the fairy's body. Decorate her wings with stars and her body with heart-shaped scraps of fabric.

7. Glue strips of fabric to the cone for legs. Stick half circles of gold card at the bottom for feet.

27

Fairy templates

Lay tracing paper over each template as needed. Hold the corners of your tracing paper in place with sticky tape before tracing around the shape.

You will need:

Tracing paper (or greaseproof paper)
Pencil
Sticky tape

A

C

D

E

F

G

29

Fairy templates

H

I

J

K

30

N

P

O

L

M

31

Fairy
Arts and Crafts

Notes for carers and teachers

These notes may be useful as a guide to the appropriate age level of each project. The suggested age is based on the difficulty of techniques used but most of the projects can be adapted to suit a variety of age levels.

Please note: adult supervision is advisable for most of these projects.